How Far is Far?

Comparing Geographical Distances

Vic Parker

www.raintreepublishers.co.uk

Visit our website to find out more information about Raintree books.

To order:

☎ Phone 0845 6044371

📄 Fax +44 (0) 1865 312263

✉ Email myorders@raintreepublishers.co.uk

Customers from outside the UK please telephone +44 1865 312262

Raintree is an imprint of Capstone Global Library Limited, a company incorporated in England and Wales having its registered office at 7 Pilgrim Street, London, EC4V 6LB – Registered company number: 6695582

Text © Capstone Global Library Limited 2011
First published in hardback in 2011
The moral rights of the proprietor have been asserted.

Edited by Nancy Dickmann, Rebecca Rissman, and Sian Smith
Designed by Victoria Allen
Picture research by Hannah Taylor
Original illustrations © Capstone Global Library 2011
Original illustrations by Victoria Allen
Production by Victoria Fitzgerald
Originated by Dot Gradations Ltd
Printed and bound in China by South China Printing Company Ltd

ISBN 978 0 431 00599 7
14 13 12 11 10
10 9 8 7 6 5 4 3 2 1

British Library Cataloguing in Publication Data
Parker, Victoria.
  How far is far? : comparing geographical distances. -- (Measuring and comparing)
  1. Distances--Measurement--Juvenile literature.
  I. Title II. Series
  530.8-dc22

Acknowledgements
The author and publisher are grateful to the following for permission to reproduce copyright material: Alamy Images pp.**5** (© Richard Levine), **24** (© Betty LaRue); © Capstone Global Library p.**4** (John Millar); © Capstone Publishers pp.**8**, **26**, **27** (Karon Dubke); Corbis p.**10** (David Zimmerman); Getty Images p.**12** (Bongarts/ Gunnar Berning); istockphoto p.**18** (© Elena Moiseeva); Photolibrary pp.**14 right**, **25** (Gunnar Kullenberg); shutterstock pp.**14 left** (© Michele Perbellini), **16** (© Marek Slusarczyk), **22** (© JCEIv).

Photographs used to create silhouettes: istockphoto, Italy (©John Woodcock); shutterstock, Great Britain (©Alfonso de Tomas), Pisa (© Oleg Babich), USA (© Dr_Flash).

Cover photograph of a road winding through wilderness reproduced with permission of Photolibrary (Ingram Publishing).

Every effort has been made to contact copyright holders of material reproduced in this book. Any omissions will be rectified in subsequent printings if notice is given to the publisher.

Contents

Words appearing in the text in bold, like this,
are explained in the glossary.

Measuring distance

Distance is how far it is from one place or thing to another. If something is near to you, you can reach it quickly. If something is far from you, you have to travel further to get to it.

When things are far in the distance, they look smaller than they really are close up.

We can use a tape measure, measuring stick, or measuring wheel to measure distances. We use centimetres (cm) to measure very short distances. Longer distances are measured in metres (m), and very long distances in kilometres (km) or miles.

As you move a measuring wheel along, the distance is shown on the handle on a digital dial.

Distances on maps

A map is a picture which shows an area shrunk down. A map can show a small area, such as your street. A map can show a larger area, such as a country.

The Earth is a ball shape, but this flat map makes it easy to look at the whole world at once.

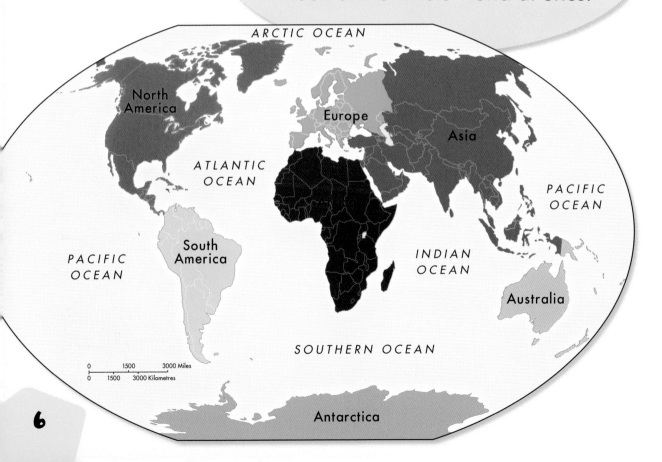

ARCTIC OCEAN

North America

Europe

Asia

ATLANTIC OCEAN

PACIFIC OCEAN

PACIFIC OCEAN

South America

INDIAN OCEAN

Australia

SOUTHERN OCEAN

0   1500   3000 Miles
0   1500   3000 Kilometres

Antarctica

On many maps, every centimetre stands for a certain number of metres or kilometres on the ground. So we can measure a distance on the map and work out how far that distance is in real life.

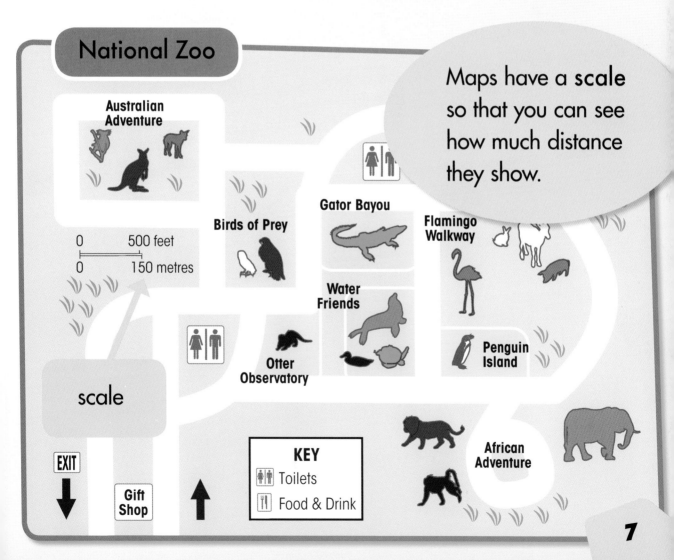

National Zoo

Australian Adventure

Birds of Prey

Gator Bayou

Flamingo Walkway

Water Friends

Otter Observatory

Penguin Island

0   500 feet
0   150 metres

scale

Maps have a **scale** so that you can see how much distance they show.

African Adventure

EXIT

Gift Shop

KEY

Toilets

Food & Drink

How far is one stride?

Have you ever measured how far you can go in one **stride**? Compared to a younger brother or sister, you can go very far. But how far is far?

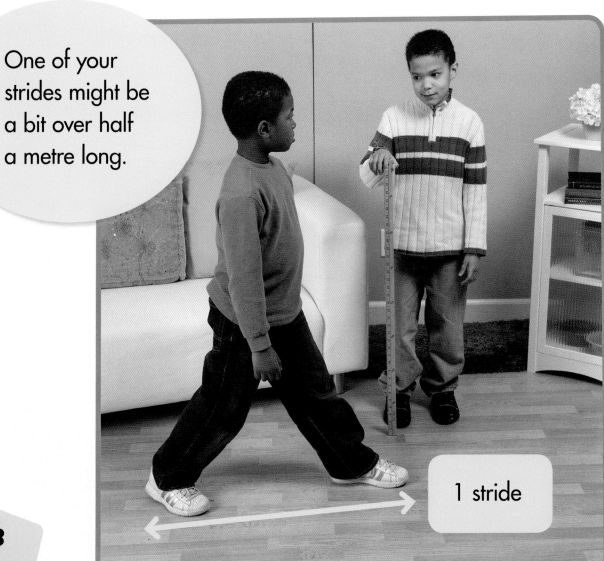

One of your strides might be a bit over half a metre long.

1 stride

The sitting room in your house might be about 6 metres wide. If you walked from one end of the room to the other, it would take about 9 strides.

1 sitting room

9 strides

What is further than walking across your sitting room?

Down a street

Streets can be long or short. When you walk down a street, you see other streets coming off from the sides. In the United States, a **block** is the distance from one side street to the next one.

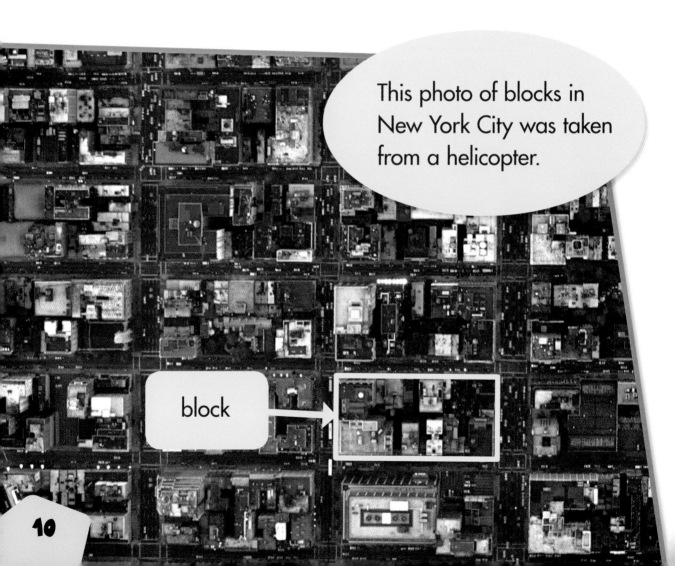

This photo of blocks in New York City was taken from a helicopter.

block

Blocks can be different lengths, but many blocks in New York City are about 80 metres long. This is a little more than 13 sitting rooms laid end to end.

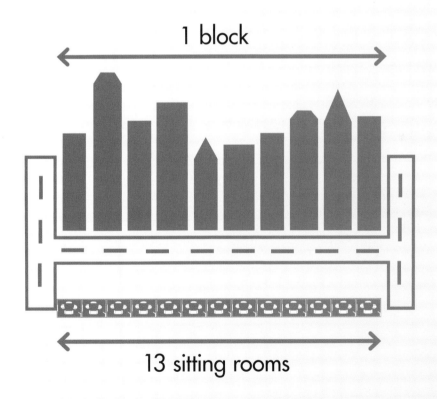

1 block

13 sitting rooms

What is further than a walk down a city street?

Along a football pitch

One end of a football pitch is far from the other. Football pitches can be different sizes. The pitches used for **international** matches must all be the same size.

Watching two countries play each other can be very exciting.

An international football pitch is 105 metres long. That is longer than a typical **block** in New York City.

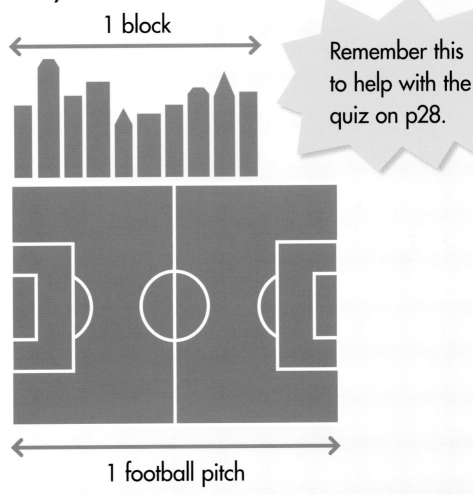

1 block

Remember this to help with the quiz on p28.

1 football pitch

What is further than walking along a football pitch? ➡

Between two cities

Travelling from one city to another is much further than walking along a football pitch. Distances this large are measured in kilometres.

Pisa

Florence

Pisa and Florence are two cities in Italy. The distance between Pisa and Florence is 69 kilometres. It would take about an hour to drive from one to the other.

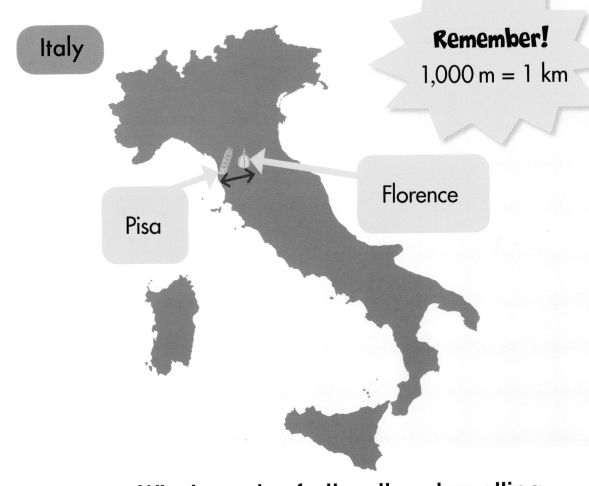

Italy

Remember!
1,000 m = 1 km

Florence

Pisa

What can be further than travelling from one city to the next? ➡

Along a mountain range

To go further than from one city to the next, you could travel from one end of a **mountain range** to another. The Pyrenees are a fairly small mountain range. They divide France and Spain.

Some parts of the Pyrenees are very snowy. Other parts are covered with thick forest.

The Pyrenees stretch about 430 kilometres from end to end. You would have to travel between Pisa and Florence more than six times to go as far as this.

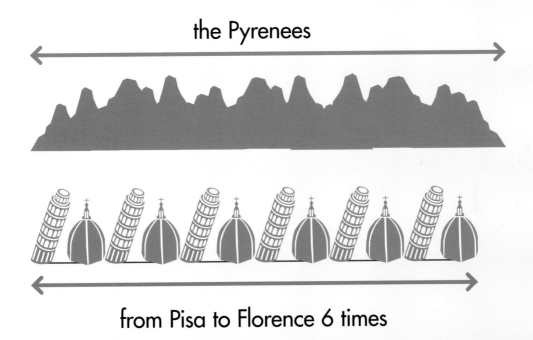

the Pyrenees

from Pisa to Florence 6 times

What can be further than travelling the length of a mountain range? ➡

The length of Great Britain

The distance from one end of the island of Great Britain to the other is longer than the Pyrenees. The distance is often measured from a village in the north called John O'Groats, to the tip of the country in the south-west, called Land's End.

This signpost is at Land's End. It is 874 miles to John O'Groats if you travel by road. That is over 1,406 kilometres.

If you went in a straight line, the distance from John O'Groats to Land's End is 970 kilometres. This is more than twice the length of the Pyrenees mountains.

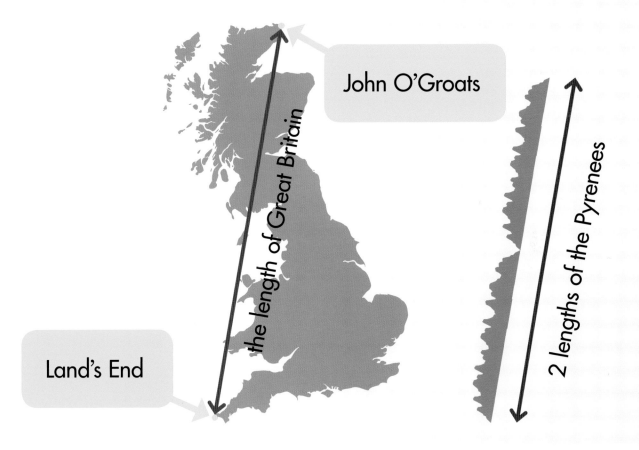

John O'Groats

the length of Great Britain

2 lengths of the Pyrenees

Land's End

What is further than travelling the length of Great Britain? ➡

The River Ganges

The Ganges is a mighty river that flows through the countries of India and Bangladesh. If you travelled the length of the River Ganges, you would have gone much further than the length of Great Britain.

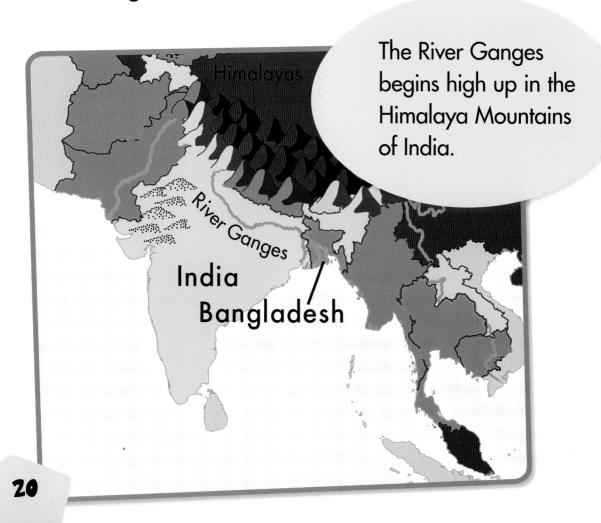

Himalayas

River Ganges

India

Bangladesh

The River Ganges begins high up in the Himalaya Mountains of India.

The River Ganges is 2,510 kilometres long, from its **source** to where it flows out into the sea. This is more than twice as far as the length of Great Britain. It is easier to see this if you show the river as a straight line.

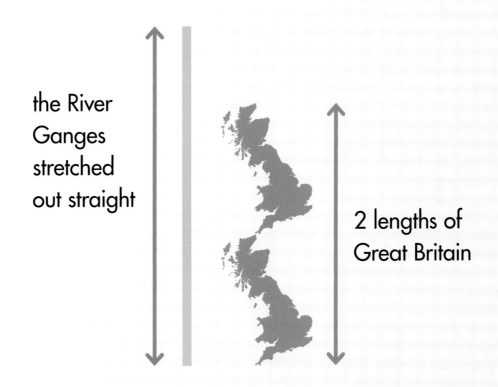

the River Ganges stretched out straight

2 lengths of Great Britain

What is further than travelling the length of the River Ganges? ➡

Across the United States

Seattle and Miami are two cities on either side of the United States. Seattle is in the **state** of Washington on the west coast. Miami is in the state of Florida, on the east coast.

Seattle

This photograph of the United States was taken from space.

Miami

Seattle and Miami are 4,388 kilometres apart. If you travelled the length of the River Ganges one and a half times, the distance between Seattle and Miami would still be further.

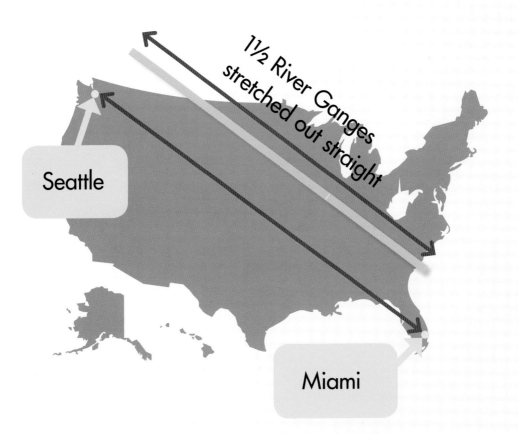

1½ River Ganges stretched out straight

Seattle

Miami

What is further than travelling across the United States? ➡

Around the world

The **equator** is an imaginary line that goes all the way around the middle of the world. If you travelled around the equator once, you would go the enormous distance of 40,075 kilometres.

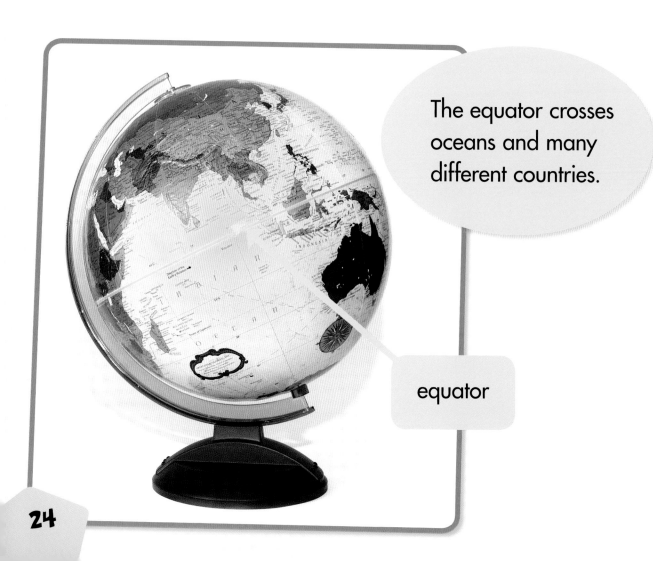

The equator crosses oceans and many different countries.

equator

The equator is more than nine times as long as the distance from Seattle to Miami. In fact, it is as far as you can go in a straight line. That is, unless you head upwards, into space!

Travelling around the world takes a long time. Most aeroplanes have to stop to **refuel** several times.

Measuring activity

Things you will need: a tape measure, a metre ruler, a pencil, and paper.

(1) Take a big **stride** and ask a helper to measure how far you stepped, in metres. Write this down so you don't forget.

(2) Stride across the longest room in your house and count how many strides it takes. Again, write your answer down.

(3) Use the length of your stride to **estimate** how far you have walked in metres.

(4) Check your answer by measuring with a tape measure. How close was your estimate?

Distance quiz and facts

Very short distances are measured in centimetres (cm).
Larger distances are measured in metres (m).
Very large distances are measured in kilometres (km).

Quiz

1. What unit would you use to measure how far it
   is from one end of your country to the other?
   a) centimetres b) metres c) kilometres

2. What unit would you use to measure how far
   a coin can go with one push?
   a) centimetres b) metres c) kilometres

3. What unit would you use to measure how far it
   is from one end of a football pitch to the other?
   a) centimetres b) metres c) kilometres

Answers: 1 = c   2 = a   3 = b

Far facts

- To travel the length of the River Nile, you would cover a distance of 6,650 kilometres. The River Nile is the longest river in the world.

- To travel the length of the Great Wall of China, you would cover a distance of 8,852 kilometres.

- If you could travel from the centre of the Earth to the centre of the Moon, you would cover a distance of 384,403 kilometres.

- If you could travel from the centre of the Earth to the centre of the Sun, you would cover a distance of about 149½ million kilometres.

Glossary

block in the United States a block is the distance from one street to the next

digital dial screen that shows numbers

equator imaginary line that runs around the middle of the Earth, halfway between the North Pole and the South Pole

estimate to use what you know to make a good guess about something's size, amount, or value without measuring it

international involving two or more countries

mountain range group of mountains

refuel vehicles need fuel to make them move. When the fuel is nearly or all used up, more fuel must be added. This is refuelling.

scale feature on a map that can be used to measure distance. A scale can show how many metres or kilometres on the ground are shown by each centimetre on the map.

source place where a river begins

state large area within a country, containing several cities and many towns and villages

stride a big, deliberate step

Find out more

Books

Follow that Map! (A First Book of Mapping Skills),
Scot Ritchie (Kids Can Press, 2009)

Maps and Mapping, Deborah Chancellor
(Kingfisher, 2006)

Reading Maps (First Guide to Maps), Daniel R. Block
and Marta Segal Block (Raintree Publishers, 2009)

Websites

www.bbc.co.uk/skillswise/e3/numbers/
measuresshapespace/length
Find out about measuring distance with the factsheet,
quiz, and measuring game on this website.

www.freemaptools.com/how-far-is-it-between.htm
Think of any two cities in the world and find out the
distance between them by using this website.

Index